LUCID LOVE

LIVE A ROMANTIC RELATIONSHIP IN A PRACTICAL WORLD

REYNOLDS BUTARI

LUCID LOVE

LIVE A ROMANTIC RELATIONSHIP IN A PRACTICAL WORLD

To my son, Noah

ACKNOWLEDGEMENTS

First of all, I thank all my therapy clients. It is through their stories that I found inspiration to write this book.

I then thank the journalists, who invited me to talk to their listeners or to write articles. They helped to highlight the usefulness of psychologists, and open the dialogue on sometimes taboo topics.

I thank my loved ones from the bottom of my heart, who believe in me and support me daily. They gave me the necessary strength by their looks, their words, their gestures and their advices, to write this book. Without them, I would not have had the courage to finish it.

I also thank all those people, whom I know personally or not, who have shown me their support and admiration for all these years. Their messages encourage me to go further and further.

Finally, thank you, dear reader, for holding this book in your hands. I hope it will add value to your love life.

Table of Contents

INTRODUCTION

I wrote this book to answer in a simple and straightforward way the questions that came up most often during my therapy sessions. Can we love two people at the same time? Can we cheat on a person we love? Is it true that all girls are materialistic? Does "real" love exist? Should I let him stay in touch with his/her ex, or should I just relax and trust him/her? Why do women forgive unfaithfulness more easily than men?

In this book, I do not only answer the questions clients asked me; I also give answers to some of the questions I asked myself during the counseling sessions.

One thing intrigued me the most when I started to really listen at my clients, especially the singles. They all had one thing in common: they had a tendency to reject automatically those who were interested in them and run after and seek those who did not seem to want them. It was still quite surprising to see how that group of wonderful singles, whether young ladies or young men, were all interested in someone who did not seem to want them. How could that be?

On the whole, they would fall in love or get attached to the "bad person." In this case, "bad person" refers to the one who does not want them in return. They all seemed to follow the same pattern: seek and follow those who do not want them and flee from those who seek them. However, they had other more interesting and more enticing alternatives, as those who sought them seemed to be interesting individuals. No matter how good-looking or attractive those wanted them seemed to be, it was never enough to change their minds; they were completely obsessed with the person who ignored and hurt them. During therapy sessions, I tried to explain and tell them they deserved better treatment than what they were receiving, and that they had a wider range of choice, but nothing seemed to convince them. The situation seemed hopeless, and the one who was interested in them had very little chance of success. He/she could be more physically attractive or smarter or richer or nicer, or more honest, but nothing helped. Their heart was "taken" by someone else who neglected or rejected them.

My clients suffered a lot, and they were ready to do anything to "win" the heart of the person who had effortlessly attracted them. In general, the person who attracted them had done it involuntarily, without seeking to know them or show any interest at all in them. It was as if there was a force emanating from that other person that had magically attracted them. As soon as they saw him/her, they sensed "instinctively" that it was the person they had always dreamed of having in their lives. They had the intimate conviction that everything had to be done to win the heart of this person. They felt that when this long-desired person would finally say "yes," they would then finally be able to experience real happiness, and they would no longer feel emptiness, loneliness or lost, which is how they normally felt inside. They were convinced that when the "yes I love you too" day arrived, they would experience a feeling of perpetual euphoria, and they would finally be able to confide and share their ideas with someone who understood and accepted them.

Of course, they were not all acting the same way. Some of them still ended up loving or being attracted in return by the person who had sought them in the beginning. Sometimes, a defining event or a small detail would change the whole setup of the game and lead them to modify the way they looked at this person they had neglected at first. The defining detail would be a circumstance that could take many forms, such as when the person was tired of being rejected and decided to move on. Or maybe the rejected person got the opportunity to go abroad in a too far-away country that would offer him/her more opportunities for the future. The defining detail could also be a career promotion, or the detail could be just that the rejected person was starting a new and serious commitment with someone else.

When those defining details were in place, the neglected person would suddenly become interesting in the eyes of my clients. They were then starting to regret they had neglected her/him in the past and were very angry at themselves. It was as if they lacked the ability to seize a good business opportunity that did not seem interesting at first sight. They had the bitter feeling they had missed their chance, and they were looking for a way to bring back under their influence that same person they had been neglecting and rejecting for so many years.

I have particularly sought to understand the origin of this tendency to always neglect the person who admires and appreciates us, regardless of his or her qualities. Why do we treat so kindly and so generously strangers or people we don't know very well but act horrible towards our loved ones? Ideally we would treat them both in a kind way, or if we had to choose between the two, then we would just do the opposite, meaning treat better and kindly those we love and ignore the strangers, right?

Indeed, we are always ready to judge in the hardest and most ruthless way the slightest misstep of our partner and he/she does the same towards us. It looks like the level of tolerance and forgiveness decreases dramatically when it comes to our partner.

I did not understand how people could spend their whole life looking for love if at the end, it meant treating her/him so unkindly once they're in "love." Why, once the euphoria of the first days has passed, do we treat each other like monsters and act more like "enemies" to each other? Why do we betray all the promises we made at the beginning of the relation-ship?

What's wrong with this idea of being in love and living as a couple? Why do many people seem so disappointed by the promises and expectations a couple's life is supposed to offers us? Why do most people give up and resign to the single idea of being happy in a couple? Why is it that, after a while, those who live in a relationship seek happiness elsewhere, away from their partner or in other activities that seem to bring them little comfort? Why do some of them end up feeling that their partner, the love of their life, has now become a mere roommate with whom they would just share the burdens and tasks of the house?

This book is, in a way, a summary of the answers I was able to find concerning all these questions that came up most often. As you go through it, you will understand why some people have simply become "chronically single" in a perpetual search for the ideal partner. Why they had multiple partners and relationships one after another trying to find the person who could "finally" suit them and fill them completely, only to be disappointed in the end. They end the relationship abruptly, or in other cases, the other ends it, and they feel wronged.

This book also contains more detailed explanations of the factors of attractions that are sold by modern society and the real factors of attraction.

I wish you all a good time reading this!

FIRST PART: THE MYTH OF IDEAL LOVE AND ITS LIMITS.

Chapter 1: The "Prince Charming" Myth.

We live in an era in which the media and the ambient culture have convinced us we have to live in a fulfilling romantic relationship if we intend to live a happy life.

Since our childhood, we are nourished by myths of charming princes and princesses who fall in love and live happily ever after. Novels, cartoons and movies portray the ideal of meeting with our "soul mate," and actors emphasize a lot about those moments of excitement and doubts of the early stage of the relationship. The actors play the moments of excitement and doubts that we feel at the moment of this meeting. Scenes in which the hero meets a stranger he doesn't know at the train station or at the airport, he finds her mysterious and appealing and then begins a quest to conquer her heart. He asks for her number, invites her to a restaurant or to a cinema, they get to know each other, and they end up declaring their passion after a few twists of events and after they have been going through some misunderstandings.

Once we become adults, we all have a secret wish to live a beautiful love story, such as those that are described in novels. We dream through a diluted myth about how relationships are supposed to be. The myth about the relationship we are supposed to live is based primarily on the meeting of two people who don't know each other at first glance, but who are destined to spend the rest of their lives together. This myth can be summarized in 11 points as follows:

1. Who is your soul mate?

Deep down inside our mind, we are convinced that in order to live a happy and fulfilling life during our short time passage on earth, we have to meet our "soul mate."

But who is your soul mate? He/she is a person that is supposed to be of great beauty inside and out, who will fill us with joy, and will stay on our side until death do us part. The myth says that if we do not have the sheer luck of meeting such a person, we will be condemned to live a life of emotional misery and loneliness as we will not have anyone to whom we can share our joys and sorrows.

But what will this person do in order to make us happy? How will we recognize him/her?

2. Love at first sight.

The myth says that the day you meet your soul mate, something inside you, a feeling or an instinct, will inform you that the person you have just "met" is not an average individual; he/she is a special person that you can't afford to miss. The feeling will be so strong, that you will feel automatically and irresistibly attracted to this person, and, in an ideal case, this will be reciprocated. You will feel accepted and desired.

If the feeling is not reciprocated, we will court him/her and undertake to seduce him/her to open her/his eyes to the possibility of such a beautiful relationship.

Nothing could block the power of that kind of relationship, not even your relatives. If they happen to disapprove the choice of our partner, or if they are not convinced by his/her profession, plans, or behavior, you can always resort to the supreme argument of modern society in terms of choice of partner: the feeling of love.

You can always tell them that you love her/him and that you knew that to be a fact from the first day you saw her/him. For sure, nobody would object to such a statement, because intuition and inner conviction are presented in fiction to be a sort of internal compass that guides each person in the choice of a partner. Modern society emphasizes the intimate conviction felt by at least one of two people at their first meeting. According to the myth, a person must respect and follow this feeling because it will help them overcome all barriers that obstruct the relationship. You are supposed to follow the voice of your "heart" and listen to your intuition, because it's the only way you will find your soul mate.

3. The Nirvana ...

The myth goes on saying that you will have more than satisfactory sex with your soul mate. Every single time, it will be akin to experiencing Nirvana, since you will be compatible and have been created for each other. What you have known with previous partners will be nothing compared to the pleasure you will feel during sex with your soul mate. It will not be a mere physical act. It is also supposed to be a kind of communion of souls and spirits, which have finally met to form one piece of the same puzzle.

4. ... An eternal pleasure...

The pleasure you will feel during sex with your soul

mate will always be on maximum level, and not only at the beginning of the relationship. This will last forever, until the end of your existence, and perhaps even into the afterlife.

If the desire decreases, it should be considered a disaster, a revealing sign that the relationship is deteriorating. You will have to find ways to revive the flame, because that kind of pleasure is only experienced with your soul mate.

5. ... and exclusive.

You'll never be sexually attracted to another person, because you have found the right/ideal partner. This partner will satisfy you fully, and you will have no drive to go elsewhere. You will feel like the shoe fits, and you will be happy and proud to stay with that person.

6. He/she will read your mind.

You will feel connected as if you are emitting on the same frequency, regardless of age, race, or level of education. Thanks to the love that unites, you'll be so connected, that you'll understand each other in in an intuitive way, without having to talk too much.

For example, he/she will guess your needs and desires, before you even have to express them. A look or a thought will suffice. He/she will be endowed with magical telepathic powers, which give him/her the ability to understand almost intuitively what you would like to say or do, and he/she will execute what we wish in order to surprise and please.

The love you share will make you want to satisfy the other person without feeling forced or coerced. He/she may even complete your sentences before you finish talking. You will share the same passions and the same values. You will finally sigh with relief as you feel understood and less alone, having finally found the person you've needed since you were born: one that can read your mind.

7. Love will guide us through the darkness.

The power of love will not only be limited to guessing the other person's thoughts. The myth sold by modern culture through fiction goes even further. It reassures you that you do not need to be educated on how to live concretely and practically in your relationship. "Listening to your heart" will be sufficient. Your only duty is to listen to your heart and intuition and they will guide you and show you how to live this relationship for the rest of your life. You do not need to know how the psychology of men or women works, because your soul mate is "supposed" to be someone unique and different from all other people. Besides, you are the only one who possesses the manual of his/her heart. He/she will also know what to do to you, and the two of you will complete each other. You were created for each other; it is supposed to be magical. You will improvise along the way, all you'll have to do is listen to your feelings, and everything will be alright, as long as the feelings are still there.

Who will pay the electricity bills? Who will prepare food? Who will pick up the children at school? Who will do the dishes, iron the clothes or do the housework? How are you going to organize the decoration of the house? Who will shower first? How will you please each other? What gift do you choose for his birthday?

All these practical questions are considered trivialities and they kill love. Fiction make us believe we will only have to follow our intuition. Our feelings will guide each of our actions and everything is supposed to play out magically. There's no need to talk about practical issues.

8. No secret or taboo between us.

You will be so united and so in love that you will be completely open to one another and will share absolutely everything, any single story without hiding anything, and it will be done without any embarrassment or fear of being judged or criticized.

There will be absolutely no secret or taboo between you and your partner. You will be able to confess and share your most secret and darkest desires, deepest wounds, dreams, ambitions, projects, disappointments, fears, and anxieties. You will be able to laugh and cry together.

You will be able to say everything that passes through your mind with the guarantee that it will remain confidential and your partner will never reveal your most intimate secrets. You will trust each other completely.

9. Living together is an endless joy.

According to the model sold by fiction, the moments spent with your soul mate will be so magical, you will wish to remain in his/her company all the time. You will experience such an amount of pleasure in spending a lot of time together, without ever getting tired. His/her presence will brighten your days as you walk in the forest or on the beach, go to the cinema, or travel together around the world sharing your schedule.

Whenever you are separated for a short period of time, however small it may be, you will feel a huge emptiness and you'll keep in touch by calling as much as possible.

10. Unconditional love.

According to this same model, that person will love you just as you are, and this unconditional love will be a true sign of love. In his/her eyes, you will be the perfect person, without any defect. If by chance he/she comes to find some flaws in you, he/she will not make much change on the intensity of her/his love and he/she will continue to love you just as you are, without demoralizing or trying to change you.

11. They lived happily ever after.

Of course, you will marry that person. The celebration of your marriage will not be like that of others. It will be different and will remain engraved in the memories. It will be an original and unique party. All those you love will be present at this ceremony: parents, uncles and aunts, cousins, childhood friends, former classmates, co-workers, etc. All will be there to share the consecration of your union. Your parents will be proud and friends will be envious.
Afterwards, you will start a family and make beautiful children who will look like two drops of water. You will give them a perfect education on which you had never talked in advance as it will come naturally.
Let's not forget that all this will be done with the same intensity of sexual and emotional passion as in

the first days of your meeting. Your lover will play several roles. She/he will be at the same time your soul mate, lover/mistress, best friend, mother/father of your children, roommate, spiritual guide, etc.

It is obvious that we feed the fantasy of a long and happy life alongside our soul mate. We also attribute to them qualities and skills that show how much our expectations are somewhat irrational. That's why many people who have tried to live this kind of romantic relationship with such a degree of expectation end up saying that love, the true one, does not exist, because they were simply disappointed. They were disappointed precisely because they expected to live this kind of relationship that we have seen in 11 points. It is the kind of love we only see in movies. But by the way, what happens at the end of the movie?

Chapter 2: When the Film Is Finished.

The myth of romantic love sold to us through novels and films often only emphasizes the meeting between these two human beings who are supposed to love each other for life. They do not explain to us how they manage to concretely live a satisfactory day-to-day relationship under the same roof in a sustainable way.

At the end of the story, the two characters are having a kiss and promise each other love and loyalty until the end of their lives, but we do not know how they will live their story.

The plot of most romantic movies is often similar. It is usually the meeting between two individuals who live a life which visibly opposes them in everything. In Titanic, Jack is a young artist of modest origin who has the chance to embark at the last minute on the most prestigious boat of the time. He meets an upper-class girl named Rose and falls in love. These two are foreign to each other, have nothing in common, do not know each other, but are irresistibly attracted to each other, thanks to the emergence of that special feeling called "love." As it happens in all romantic love stories, at the beginning, they have to overcome some obstacles that get in the middle of their path. These obstacles can take the form of a misunderstanding, a malicious competitor, the disapproval of family or close friends, distance, social status or simply the level of education. Our two lovers do everything to pass the tests together, take the opportunity to strengthen their union against these challenges, and usually end up swearing love to each other. But we don't get to know the rest of the story; we are left guessing how they will spend that happy life together. Nobody explains to us how these two people con-cretely go about living and maintaining their relation-ship. Moreover, in the great classics of romantic love stories, such as Romeo and Juliet, the two lovers die at the end, so we have no concrete and practical indi-cation of how they would live such an inflamed rela-tionship. In the cases where they survive, we are told this special feeling called "love," which is at the origin of their union, will be enough to keep them happy together. It is implied that as long as this feel-ing will be present, their relationship will be strong until the end of their life. When we watch these movies, it seems like the only ingredient we really need for a satisfying relationship is love. The rest does not matter, since the majority of fiction stops when the two characters say "Yes! I love you too!"

Expectations are so high when it comes to romantic relationships. We put so much pressure on ourselves that as soon as our relationship does not look like those described in the movies, we naively believe we chose the wrong partner and we will not make it as a couple.

Why are many people convinced that they made the right choice at first but regret it bitterly afterwards? Did this special feeling mislead them?

Chapter 3: The Myth Has Limits.

Few of us can claim to have a relationship as described in Chapter 1. Many have tried but ended up disappointed and bitter, even claiming love simply does not exist. So, what's going wrong in this case?
In reality, the myth of romantic love is based on impractical concepts, which we will discuss here.

1. The perfection of the loved one.

The myth states that the person who is supposed to share our life has special abilities. He/she will want us physically all the time, every day, no matter what are our attitude towards her/him. Their love will be unconditional.
We believe that if someone really loves us, he/she

should love us "just as we are." Even if we have some flaws, this should not count, our partner is supposed to tolerate and support them as a sign of love. We do not accept the advice of our lover, and we especially do not want him/her to tell us to change this or that behavior. We take their advice as insults or as a mark of judgment.

So goes our reasoning: "How dare they tell me I have to change? If they really loves me, they will excuse me and tolerate me. If they do not find that I am perfect, it is because they do not love me. Their love should be unconditional."

We also hope that if our partner really loves us, they can read our minds and be able to guess our needs. Not only can they guess our thoughts, but they execute our wishes without us even asking. We interpret this ability to guess our desires and read our thoughts as a sign of love.

We think of someone to whom we can openly confide without any fear of being ridiculed. Someone who has unlimited patience and an incredible listening ability.

But where does this need come from? Why do we want to meet someone who can love us unconditionally? Why do we yearn for someone who would treat us like babies or toddlers by constantly guessing and providing our needs?

The answer is in the question itself. The keywords are "babies" and "toddlers."

This need comes at the very beginning of our lives, when our parents or those who took care of us gave us what we needed. Our parents or caregivers loved us unconditionally, guessed our needs and responded to them even though we didn't know what we really wanted. All we needed to was cry, because that's all we knew and could do at the time, and they would struggle to guess and meet every need we had. At the same time, our needs were not so various. At the time, we just needed to be entertained, eat and sleep. That's why our parents, or those who took care of us at the time, could easily guess what our needs were. Everything was done without any effort on our part; our only duty was to cry and everything was settled.

On top of that, they forgave all our mistakes, because we were still small and we were not aware of the consequences of our actions. We could break a glass, refuse to eat, throw food on the ground, and cry all night, and our parents did not hold it against us. They forgave us and continued to love us unconditionally. We did not need to make an effort or love them in return; they just loved us. Our presence was enough to make them happy. We only had to play or laugh to make them feel satisfied.

This first experience of "love" we had with those who took care of us when we were young deeply marks our perception of love, and we project it on our adult relationships. It's not very helpful because it creates an unrealistic expectation of what it is to be loved. How can we realistically believe that once adult, we can have someone who is going to love us constantly and tirelessly, if we don't make any effort to please them in return? How could anyone guess our adult needs, with all the nuances of our moods, goals, values and motivations? Unfortunately, when we come across a partner who is not ready to listen to all the details of how we spend our day, because he/she is also a human being who is tired after a long day of frustrating work, and he/she doesn't marvel at each of our small gestures, as our parents did, we could wrongly feel with regret that we are not being loved. We just have to recognize that our partners are not unskilled and unable to pay attention; the drama is that we judge them with our adult experience in comparison to the best moments we got from childhood.

In reality, we become angry against our partners when they don't guess our needs and desires, or read our minds. And when our partner asks us what's wrong, we answer: "It's okay, everything is fine." We believe it is our partner's role and duty to find out why we are frustrated, without any explanation from our side.

Now that we are grown up and adults, it would be very illusory to believe that another adult could give us the same kind of unconditional love we have received from our parents. We should admit that we are not perfect and that our faults are sometimes a limitation to the development of our relationship. We should let our partners enlighten us and advise us on our many flaws, and start the background work to better enjoy our relationship.

2. The strength of the feeling of love.

There is a kind of "illiteracy" in romantic relationships, because we generally believe the mere presence
of love is enough to have a successful relationship. As
we will see later in this book, the feeling of love is
much more complex than what we think, and it can't
be the only ingredient of a harmonious couple.
When it comes to romantic relationships, we base our
judgment on our intuition. Sometimes, we meet a
beautiful stranger in the street, then we set fire on our
imagination and start to make a self-produced movie
in our mind about his/her qualities. A look, a smile, a
way of walking, will be enough to produce in us an
intimate conviction that "this time, it is the one." We
will call that sudden conviction a "special feeling"
afterwards. Then we begin to imagine how lucky we
would be and how happy we would feel if this special
person ever came to love us in return. Here, we are
conquered in a few minutes and ready to commit ourselves forever with a perfect stranger.
We have to understand that the role played by feelings is not sufficient enough to keep the people in
love together. Both partners need to make construc-
tive efforts. It is not enough to hope that everything
will be fine without providing any effort. There are
things we have to put into action in order to achieve
our goals.

Chapter 4: A Mentality of Lack at the Origin of the Myth.

The cultural and social environment in which we live determines the choice of our spouses, the people to whom we are attracted, and it significantly influences the way we treat those who live with us.

For example, we are often attracted to people who are inaccessible and out of reach, and we tend to idealize those who attract us. At first, we think our partner will be perfect, but once we are in the relationship, we neglect and treat them wrongly, because we take them for granted.

In order to understand where the lack mentality comes from, we have to keep in mind how much the capitalist model conditions us to love winners, heroes, and the disciplined, free-minded, self-made man. Let's go deep in details on how this capitalist model conditions our attractions and how it defines those we dream of and who attract us.

1. The measure of success: the envy and the gaze of others.

The capitalist worldview drives us to envy those who possess things of great value. According to this worldview, these things boil down to the three fundamentals of capitalism: money, popularity, and power.

Modern society teaches us to measure our success based on how others look at you. You will know that you have succeeded if others envy who you are or what you have. The way people look at you will be an indicator of success.

Thus, if a large number of people envy you, want to be in your place or want to acquire the things you own, it will mean they are valuable. On the contrary, if no one envies you or your things or situation, it will mean it has no value. For example, it is widely agreed that we can measure the success of a particular movie, show or book if it has been seen or read by a large number of people.

Since other people's view has become a measure of success, we often apply the same principle in the choice of our partner. We tend to choose the one who will attract us, but most importantly convince our family or close friends. In other words, we are looking for a partner who can create envy in the eyes of others. It makes us appreciate him/her ten times more.

2. Things of value are rare and scarce.

Modern society has taught us to believe that things of great value are scarce and limited in quantity (gold, diamonds, luxury cars, high-paying jobs, fancy restaurants, etc.). Almost all the things our capitalist society values have one thing in common: they are rare and in very limited quantities. They are therefore not accessible to the "average" because they can't afford it, as it becomes too expensive.

We grew up with the illusion that anything that has real value is very rare and scarce, and we will really have to "pay a high price" in order to acquire it.

Of course, the price to pay depends on the nature of the valued thing we want to acquire. We know, for example, that if we want a degree to pursue a prestigious profession, the price will be many years of study. We also know that fancy restaurants are not only rare, but they are above all very expensive and do not welcome anyone.

Unfortunately, we apply this worldview to relationships and transpose the same conclusions.

3. People of value are rare and limited in quantity.

Sometimes, we reject those who want to be in a romantic relationship with us because we think they are wrong about us. We think they are blind and do not see how uninteresting we are. Some of us believe we do not deserve so much attention because we are not so extraordinary. We think these people are totally wrong about us, and do not know how empty and useless we are. We are scared that we may get busted as a fraud once we are in the relationship and they discover who we really are. So, we deliberately choose to reject them, because we fail to accept that we can be interesting.

On the other hand, we are looking for our soul mate with the idea that we will struggle for years to find "the right" person with whom we will share our life. We think of it as a struggle, a busy and terrifying road full of danger and obstacles. In our mind, finding the "right" person must be a real challenge. We think one must suffer as much as he/she suffers to find an ideal, well-paying and exciting job.

That mindset results in terrible outcomes. When someone is interested in us, we think he/she is not the "right one" because it does not correspond to our capitalist worldview, which says we have to struggle first. It says we have to run behind the "right one," the same way we run after great opportunities. We are rather attracted by people who show us no sign of interest or accessibility.

We therefore assume that a person who "offers" himself/herself so easily is not very valuable. We think there must be something wrong going on. What does he/she really want? Why me? That's why we refuse their advances. Our reasoning is: "If those people who are interested in us were really worthy, it would be us and the rest of the world chasing after them, not the other way around."

"Precious things are rare and limited in quantity." When this logic is transposed to love relationships, those who are most willing to show signs of affection suffer the most. Whoever receives these marks of affection perceives them as a sign of weakness.

So, how do we attract the person who attracts us? Here again, modern society tells us we have to go through a long and painful process of seduction, which follows a simple logic: you have to become someone exceptional to possess something exceptional.

4. Seduction: the heavy price to pay to appear exceptional and find love.

According to modern society, if we are single and alone, it is entirely our fault. We are supposed to do something to resolve this situation if we're not happy with it.

Modern society tells us that we are not yet interesting enough to attract people to us the way we are now. So, it tries to find reasons for our aloneness: we are ugly, fat, or just not physically attractive; our haircut is not pretty or our approach is not dynamic enough. This gives the impression that we are not ambitious people. We get rejected because we are not interesting enough to attract the right people. Sometimes, we even feel like they are avoiding us.

The general idea is that if we change or repair two or three little things, we will become extraordinary and exceptional people who can attract other interesting people.

When we get into that kind of mindset, we are ready to do anything possible to please others. It becomes our first priority to find out and fix the "wrong thing" in us.

At first sight, this equation seems logical and seductive. Many of us usually stick to it. Facing the peril of spending the rest of our lives alone, we decide to act and change. To make this happen, we put all the probabilities on our side, and we do everything to hide our flaws and vulnerabilities.

We start a long journey to the path of perfection ... We check our look, we do everything to show we are successful (especially men), we correct our posture (especially women), we learn to speak in a more suitable language, we adopt techniques to send captivating text messages, etc. At the end of the day, we are trying to become perfect, because we are convinced that love is a response to perfection.

My opinion is, people should stop torturing themselves for nothing. Nobody is perfect! Some people have far worse faults than ours and are already in a relationship with those we consider gods and goddesses.

If someone thinks that they are not interesting because they are overweight, then they should remember that there are people who are way bigger and fatter than they are who have already found a partner. If a young man thinks he's single because he does not have a penny, he should know there are younger and more poverty-stricken guys than him who are in beautiful relationships.

In fact, no matter what the reason or the weakness that society will find for us in order to justify our condition of celibacy, we must keep in mind there will always be someone who is worse than us but has managed to find a partner.

There is no need to be perfect to find love. If we want to lose a few pounds, to go to church, to fix our look or to improve our language, we have to do it for the right reasons. We have to do it first for ourselves and for our well-being to feel better about ourselves; it should not be seen as a means to finding a partner.

5. Why do we idealize the people who attract us?

Primarily, we idealize people who attract us because we believe love is the answer to perfection. We believe anyone worthy of our love should necessarily inspire our admiration and fascination, as well as those around us. Our modern society, governed by capitalist values, pushes us to idealize those who "succeed" and to denigrate the "losers".

Society encourages us to choose what is best for us. For example, if we want to buy a new car, we will spend an infinite time on the Internet comparing the different choices offered. We do the same at the restaurant where we try to select the best food experience from the menu.

This idea of seeking the best for oneself has been transmitted to us by the capitalist worldview. It promotes competition within companies, so they can offer the "best choice" to consumers. We apply the same capitalistic principle in our love relationships. We look for the best partner within our reach, whether on dating sites or in our direct environment. Our imagination has been shaped so we are attracted by people who have special abilities.

Is there any harm in wanting to find the best partner?

On the surface, no. The problem is that in terms of romantic relationships, we always end up being disappointed and frustrated by our choices. The ideal partner, Prince Charming or our soul mate, is less flamboyant, full of imperfections, and much less adequate than we imagined the first time we met.

It is said that love makes you blind. This is true in a certain sense. Sometimes, the passion we feel for those who attract us makes us blind to their imperfections. We are so fascinated and charmed that we forget one small fact: they are normal human beings with qualities and flaws.

In short, we confuse causes and effects. Indeed, we are not charmed and attracted because they are perfect. On the contrary, it is rather because we are in love that we keep a certain idea of perfection about them and do not see their flaws, particularly since we fall easily and quickly under the spell of strangers.

6. But why do we idealize strangers so much?

Strangers are easier to romanticize.

It is easier to fantasize about them; we can easily imagine their supposed qualities and play with our own imagination.

The image (see Chapter 1) we create about them is based on a few, sometimes minimal, elements that we noticed about them. These elements can be the watch they wear, the delicacy of their fingers, the color of their hair, the intensity of their eyes, the way they hold a glass of wine, etc.

Our close friends, or close relatives, are not as lucky because we are conscious of their limitations and some of their weaknesses. We can't manage to project an idea of perfection on them, because our imagination is limited by the reality and the weight of the daily life that we undergo together with them. Our imagination blossoms more easily in front of strangers, whether they are people, places, or even objects. It is also for this reason that in order to win in the game of seduction, it is important to keep a mysterious side that makes us look charming in the eyes of others.

Then comes this question: what tells us that this stranger is the "right person"? Where does this conviction come from?

7. The reign of intuition.

The power of intimate conviction is put in the foreground. When our close relatives disapprove of the choice of our partner, maybe because they are not convinced by his profession or his plans, we will always be able to resort to the supreme argument of the modern society on the matter of partner choice: the feelings of love. We can always justify our choice by saying we deeply love that person, and we knew it from the first time we laid our eyes on her/him.

No one will oppose such a statement. It works because intuition and inner conviction are presented in fiction as the internal compass that will guide us in the choice of our partner. Modern society highlights this intimate conviction, felt by at least one of the two people the first day they meet. Fiction says we must respect this feeling and overcome all the obstacles that could block this relationship. We're supposed to listen to the voice of our "heart," and follow our intuition. Those two are supposed to help us find our soul mate.

The approach of inner conviction was adopted in opposition to the marriage of reason, which implied that families bring together two individuals in marriage who will help to acquire or preserve different privileges.

It is amazing how this approach to inner conviction is radical, dangerous and ineffective because it takes into account only one factor: the feeling generated at the time of the encounter. This approach ignores the practical aspects of life. Yet, statistics show that these practical aspects are the source of many disputes and separations.

But then, how do we manage to live these relationships, in which we decide to engage with perfect strangers, on the basis of an intuition or a feeling?

8. The myth of the inaccessible: source of frustration.

Our capitalistic modern society has produced individuals who do not appreciate what they possess. On the contrary, it has conditioned us to desire and envy what we do not possess.

The capitalist system needs two types of individuals: producers and consumers. The first category is made up of a minority of individuals who produce consumer goods for a mass of consumers. In order to sell their products to consumers, manufacturers bombard us with advertisements that draw us to want and need their products from a very young age.

Manufacturers compete ingenuously to convince us that we will never be really happy if we do not buy a particular product. To push us to buy, advertisers seek to create frustration in us, convincing us by all means necessary that we need their product. Modern capitalist society arranges to produce individuals frustrated by their lives, for it is only at this price that the economy can function normally.

So, we grew up with the illusion that we will never be happy or satisfied by the things we already possess. We think that happiness is found in the next gadget we see in a commercial or watch in the latest movie released in the cinema. In the long run, we have upheld a belief that happiness is found in things we do not own or cannot acquire. We are craving things we don't have and we are attracted to those who have or are the things we are craving for or wish to be. We think we can only find satisfaction outside of ourselves, so we constantly contemplate the outer world hoping it will bring better things than we already have.

When we were still young children, we were influenced by the toys and cakes we saw in store windows or on TV. Thus, we grew up in a world where we could not be happy as long as we did not own this or that toy. The more this toy was inaccessible, the more it was valuable to us.

This conditioning has led us to crave for the things we don't have and neglect and denigrate those we already have. Once grown-up, these toys become big cars, big houses, and beautiful holidays on distant paradise islands, big bank accounts, and popularity.

It is not surprising that with such conditioning, many people can't fully appreciate their already existing relationship. They constantly compare themselves to other couples and constantly question their choice. These people live as if their relationship is a burden and take their partner for granted. They hope that in the future, they will meet another person who will finally make them happy. They spend all their energy daydreaming of the day when they meet this stranger and fantasize about his supposed qualities, to the point they forget to improve their current reality.

Second part:

What are the factors of attraction?

To explain the attraction factors, I'm not going to rely on purely superficial forms, such as "I like smart, slim girls with long hair" or "I prefer mature men with abs, with a true stable career." I propose instead to get to the bottom of the subject.

I would like to address the reasons that lead us to choose "this" person among all these slim and intelligent girls and among all those tall and handsome men. What makes him/her prevail over all others? What is this "special little thing" that makes him/her so different from others and so special to us?

In this part, I will outline all the factors of attraction that define who we choose to live with. I divided these different factors into three categories: 1) those put forward by the capitalist value system, 2) those based on "moral values," and 3) the real or factual ones.

Chapter 1: Attraction Factors Given by Modern Society.

In general, we are attracted to those who have what we do not have. We have discussed this in detail in earlier chapters, but it is important to keep in mind this one thing: we have an almost unhealthy appeal to people who have access to what we have not been able to get. We find their life wonderful, because we are convinced they do not live our frustration. We overestimate their abilities and attribute excessive qualities to them.

Modern society shapes us through stories, novels and films to convey to us a certain concept of love, according to which one can't speak of love without referring to Prince Charming.

1. The concept of Prince Charming.

Have you ever wondered why the fairy tales of our childhood only talked about princes, queens, kings, or other people with a high social status? It is rare that we are told the story of the baker's son who marries the blacksmith's daughter.

Beauty and the Beast, Sleeping Beauty, Cinderella, Snow White and the Seven Dwarfs, The Snow Queen ... all these titles are children's stories that shape their imagination. In these tales, boys are incited to become worthy charming princes in the service and comfort of their beautiful princess.

The tone is set at a very early stage. To be attractive, boys learn they have to get some sort of power, no matter what form it takes. And girls must have grace, youth, innocence, and beauty, no matter what form it will take in real life.

What are these traits of power and beauty impressed through the tales of modern culture? What image should be conveyed by boys and girls who fascinate and attract us?

2. The 5 characteristics of Prince Charming and the modern princess.

When someone wants to be admired, according to current social criteria, they must generally have at least one of the following 5 characteristics. Let us note first that the candidate may miss 4 of these 5 characteristics, but he/she must compensate intensively and proportionally by one of them, which will make him/her remarkably attractive.

a. Physical beauty.

Physical beauty is one of the five characteristics the person who attracts us must present. It is defined according to different criteria within different cultures, but some criteria are almost universal.

In general, for men, physical beauty is expressed by physical force, represented by an athletic body. In our subconscious, male physical strength is a form of protection against potential danger. An athletic body also symbolizes an idea of perseverance, discipline and self-control, since everyone knows that to achieve this, one must go through hours of exercise and have a mind of steel. Broad shoulders, a muscular torso and a square chin are signs of good physical health.

For women, however, physical beauty is expressed by a face that has fine and symmetrical features ("baby face" style), plus fine hands and feet. These soft and warm features represent the tenderness and comfort that reassures men. Other physical characteristics, such as the size of breasts, buttocks, legs, and hips, and the shape of the back or the neck, are signs of fertility, which pull a strong attraction from men, depending on their ideals of beauty.

Thus, in general, the criteria of physical beauty in men are square shapes, while in women, it will be rounded shapes.

b. Financial success.

Financial success, or being born from a wealthy and affluent family, is also a factor of attraction. This fascination we have for financial success, which is in some ways taboo, is brought up by two of the most ancestral fears that we all have in common: the fear of extinction and the loss of autonomy.

Financial success protects us from need and the stress of doing a job we do not like just to earn a small salary at the end of the month. Those who are financially independent are perceived as privileged people who have freedom to use their time as they wish, and they have no limitations in acquiring or doing whatever they want.

A promising and high potential for future success can also help pull attraction. Sometimes, we can be attracted to someone just because he/she has a very promising future in business.

This case is to be considered as pure speculation. Instead of being with someone who is already rich, we engage with someone in the hope of what he/she may become one day. It is therefore a form of risk management that is similar to stock market speculation.

c. Social influence.

Sometimes, we are attracted to people we find "cool" on the basis that they have found grace in the eyes of others. They are people who enjoy a certain charisma with their peers. They are listened to, appreciated and admired within their circle, such as the university, the church, the office, the social networks, the media, a political party, and so on.

Generally, we trust the judgment of others. It is no wonder that we are attracted to someone who is appreciated by others, especially if we share the same values as this group of people who appreciate him/her.

In short, a person can attract us because they have this one trait: a social status that gives them access to a wide network of friendship and support.

d. Be a high achiever in a career or hobby.

Reaching the peaks in any career is also a feature that attracts others. It can be a career in any field: sports, music, military, academia, politics, art, cinema, finance, computer science, etc. Regardless of the chosen career, the surrounding culture prompts us to admire those who become champions in their field.

Talented people and those successful in their field attract crowds of admirers, so they exert an even more powerful attraction to us, since they bring together two characteristics of attraction: a high position and social influence.

But where does this mentality of admiring high achievers come from? During childhood, the school system encourages competition, and teaches the young child that he/she will be loved and valued by the world only if he/she becomes the first in class. In return, parents promise rewards if he excels at school. What stays in the child's mind? The child keeps in mind that in order to be loved enough, he must win the competition against his classmates. It's the only way he will be valued in society and make his parents proud, who are at this time his only source of love. Thus, once grown up, he/she will fight for a success-ful career to be valued and to pull attraction.

e.   Be of great intelligence.

Someone who holds an intelligent, charismatic, sub-stantial and logical speech ends up arousing some form of admiration. Intelligence represents in modern times what muscles represented in prehistoric times. Someone who is intelligent, wise, and smart has not only a better chance for survival, but also a better means of adaptation to this ever-changing world that is running on a speed very difficult to catch. By living alongside an intelligent person, we believe we will be better advised and safe from bad decisions and their consequences.

f. Conclusion on the 5 characteristics of the Prince Charming and the modern Princess.

Of course, few people fulfill these five characteristics put forward by modern society. The full satisfaction of the 5 characteristics is often reserved for celebrities, politicians, athletes, or artists. In general, we are in a relationship with "normal" people whom we would be ready to leave immediately if ever any of the celebrities wanted us. But we are aware of the low probability this will happen to us one day. So, we try to project on our partners a potential of one these 5 characteristics, which they could have in the future.

But then, what do we do to find a "normal" partner? What is our selection criteria? Why do we choose one partner over another?

Chapter 2: Who Are These Charming Princes and Princesses of Modern Times?

We spend most of our adult life looking for a kind of happiness that can be summed up in three simple words: popularity, power and money. But in modern times, the search for happiness has added a fourth component: finding love.

By finding love we mean we are looking for someone who can share our ups and downs in addition to help us achieve happiness. We are looking for a person who has this "little thing" that we miss to complete our life and make it totally perfect. Someone who has or represents one of the three components (popularity, power and money) that our society has enacted, but who, at the same time, will make us feel admired, appreciated and important.

Sometimes, we do not have any of these three components. We are neither popular, rich nor powerful. So, we project one of these attributes on the person who attracts us. He/she becomes like the star of our life.

As we saw in the previous section, in love as in life, we are attracted to people who possess what we do not have and crave for. We admire them even more when we have the impression that these people have not made any effort to acquire that thing or quality we think we'll never get.

1. Free and independent heroes.

We live in a time when the peak of personal accomplishment means being autonomous and independent. Modern society has established independence and autonomy as trophies we must reach to finally enjoy happiness. We bought into that theory, and all of us aspire to a form of freedom and independence in various areas of life.

Areas vary indeed. Sometimes, we want to free ourselves from heavy social limitations imposed by a certain standard of living. Or, freedom may mean that we would like to achieve some financial independence, not to have to go to work each morning and instead do what we really love. In any case, we believe freedom and independence are the prerequisites for thriving and enjoying life. We believe that with these two elements, we could do the things we love, and thus make our lives much more enjoyable.

According to the image conveyed by modern society, a successful person is autonomous and doesn't need anyone. It is someone who has achieved a lot of things alone, a resourceful person who manages to do things alone, without seeking help.

Our society evolves in the myth of the "self-made man," according to which the hero is independent of everything. He has managed to make millions without the help of anyone. In everyday life, this hero is a "do-it-yourselfer" who knows how to do everything, alone, at home.

A modern-time Prince Charming is therefore a hero who is in control. Unlike Walt Disney's Prince Charming, who "inherited" his privileges, the modern Prince Charming must provide discipline and hard work without the help of anyone to achieve and win a privileged life. This is why reality shows, television series and other high-budget films often feature heroes who know how to get out of difficult situations on their own, without calling for help.

The context in which we live encourages us to love and desire freedom. Thus, we admire these free and independent women and men, because independence and freedom are considered the attributes of a sexy and cool person.

This idea of the free and independent hero who is in control of everything that surrounds him/her is at the root of several dramas in romantic relationships. In fact, couples, or those who aspire to find love, are constantly trying to play free and independent heroes, and they end up disappointed and disillusioned because living and succeeding in a couple relationship often requires a person to lose some form of freedom and independence.

Indeed, the requirements and obligations involved in the choice of having a couple relationship strongly contrast with the ideal of freedom and independence defended by modern society.

The root of the problem lies in the fact that we are often told about fabulous and heroic stories in which they forget to mention that behind every individual success, there is a social context to justify and explain the result.

2. The hero and his team.

Basically, what is disturbing to the myth maintained by our modern society is that we often tend to put the "hero" in the spotlight, and we forget about "the team" behind his/her success. Thus, by constantly being exposed to messages highlighting these exceptional individuals, capable of accomplishing feats without any particular assistance, we unconsciously seek to look like them.

However, we often forget to mention, for example, that even the greatest athletes have coaches, doctors, sponsors, and a whole lot of support, which plays a big role and contributes to their success. Or, we forget that the big American billionaires would not have become one if they were born and grew up in North Korea.

This "forgetfulness" is therefore at the root of the tragedy of today's society. Everyone wants to live his life as an autonomous and independent "hero" because the ideal to achieve is to achieve all alone.

3. The difference between the modern hero and the Middle Age hero.

We face a paradox of a particular nature. On one hand, our human nature, our inner self, drives us to seek and desire connection with other people. This desire for intimacy is so powerful that we feel incomplete until we find the "ideal" person. On the other hand, we want to look like our modern heroes. We want to prove that we don't need anyone, and we want to be applauded and admired by the whole world, whom we admire in return.

Unlike the heroes of the Middle Ages ready to fight against the worst monsters to save their princess, the current hero doesn't need anyone. He does not need the princess's kiss to feel validated and loved. Our modern-day hero has other more important concerns. He/she must serve the world for a greater cause, fight to defend the environment, or save the political world. The real difference between the ancient and modern hero lies in their attachment style. Indeed, the hero of the Middle Ages is anxious at the idea of not seeing his sweetheart again. He is not afraid to show signs of attachment, and he wants to prove his love as well as his value. He does not hesitate to run to the rescue of his sweetheart to prove his affection. The feeling of love felt for her is the source of motivation. He puts himself in considerable danger simply because he is attached to her. The hero of the Middle Ages falls in love and seeks the reciprocity from the gracious and tender loved woman. He will probably be chosen among several other men who are competing to win her heart.

Meanwhile, the modern hero doesn't fall in love or get attached so easily. He has an avoidance approach toward feelings. When he takes risks, it's because he is devoted to a cause, not because he is in love or try-ing to impress a girl. The modern hero arouses the admiration of all, and all the girls of the city dream of him. He is a star. His only task is to make a choice between all those who admire him. He is the one who chooses among several candidates; he does not fight to be accepted, and he does not need to prove his val-ue. He will eventually meet one while he is saving or helping the world. The cherished person is not the cause that inspires the action of the hero.

4. The modern hero does not cling.

The people who attract us are often those who seem to be able to do well without us. It looks like they have a life that seems so interesting and exciting, that they won't have any time to think of "average people" like us. These people are so busy fighting important struggles for the good of humanity that it would be an honor for them to speak to us.
Thus you understand why we have an annoying tendency to automatically brush-off anyone who shows interest and availability for us. As soon as a person becomes accessible, available and interested, we denigrate him/her, because it does not correspond to the image conveyed by society: "He/she needs me? Then it means he/she is not the hero/heroine I imagined.
Our hero is one who does not seek love because he does not need it. People love him desperately, while he/she loves humanity in general. Attaching him/herself to one person would mean sacrificing the energy, time and financial means he was supposed to devote to his/her important mission.
But where does this idea that someone who needs love is the opposite of a hero come from? Why do we lack respect for those who "need" us, need our love and our presence? Why are we allergic to addiction and all those who might depend on us?

5. Why looking for love is perceived as a sign of weakness?

When someone tries to seduce us, we interpret it as a tell-tale sign of despair. Then we run away from them as we run away from the beggars in the street, because in our eyes, they are beggars of love. Once again, we are transposing our capitalist worldview on relationships. We think we would lose if we got into this relationship because these "beggars" do not have much to offer in real life or in love.

In general, we run away from beggars of all kinds, because they represent two concepts we all try to avoid: dependence and neediness.

We live in a society that loathes addiction. It is often presented to us as a failure. Indeed, it contains in it a negative connotation. When we think of addiction, we automatically think of destructive behavior.

The form of addiction that immediately comes to our minds is the dependence on so-called "addictive" substances, such as alcohol, cigarettes, and other illicit drugs. We also think of gambling addiction as a deviant and harmful behavior for us and our entourage. We think of certain fathers ruined by sports betting, or of people who have lost everything in one evening at the casino, and who have no idea how to stop hurting themselves.

We define addiction as a loss of control. It's when we cannot do without something anymore, a kind of morbid addiction, where we no longer have control over our craving or our need to smoke, drink or play at the casino.

It is therefore legitimate that modern society invites us to keep control of our minds and actions. For example, no parent would want his child to fall under the influence of drugs.

But what is the kind of addiction we are most afraid of? Why, for example, is every parent afraid that his child will become addicted to drugs? Beyond the issues of mental and physical health, what's really wrong and problematic with addiction?

What is problematic for each parent is that their child is at risk for two forms of addiction. On the one hand, there is the risk of becoming dependent on the substances a person consumes. But on the other hand, he risks remaining dependent on his parents and his entourage to provide for his primary needs, such as accommodation and food. Thus, the parent would easily accept that his child becomes dependent on substances, as long as he/she is able to make a living. Indeed, every parent wants his child to grow, develop and be able to support himself/herself.

Dependence on other human beings is the one that is the most embarrassing, regardless of the context. Whether internationally or individually, this principle applies in the same way. For example, each country tries to gain some form of autonomy and independence from other countries. On the individual level, each person is looking for a way to depend as little as possible on others.

Just think of how difficult it is for you to seek help or ask for a service. Remember how complicated it is to ask someone for money, and the feeling of being downgraded and diminished in your esteem every time you do it. We would rather prefer to program machines and applications to meet our needs rather than go ask another human being.

According to modern society, asking someone for help, needing or depending on someone, is considered a failure. Indeed, modern society, with its materialistic and individualist vision of the superhero, indirectly invites us to denigrate any person in a situation of dependence. This mentality drives us to look at anyone in a situation of dependency as an inferior, unfitted, or anti-hero. The beggars, the poor, the refugees, and all the other people in a situation of financial dependence pay the price of this vision of the world.

The solution offered by our capitalist society is to do everything possible to get money. If we succeed, we will not "need" anyone, so we will avoid the humiliation of beggars and others. With money, we will preserve our dignity and independence. We will be able to dress, lodge, move and gain in respectability.

This is true in many contexts of social life, but not in the context of romantic relationships, because feelings change the game. Money can attract potential partners, but it does not solve a major problem. No matter what we do, we will always need a certain person to love us in return and show us sincere and genuine signs of affection.

6. In love, beggars and kings are all equal.

There is a difference between "successful career" and "successful life."

A successful career refers to professional success. It can mean succeeding in one's career, progressing in one's social status, and feeling more respected, more integrated, more dignified and, indeed, safer from "necessity." This is when we no longer need our parents or the state to provide for our needs. With professional success, we feel inhabited by a sense of independence from society. We become free and independent heroes in the eyes of society.

"Succeeding in life" refers to our sense of personal happiness. It is to be filled on the intimate level, to succeed in relations maintained with our spouse, children, parents, etc. More generally, it is to succeed in maintaining good quality interactions with the people around us. It is to supplement emotional needs and feel fulfilled in return.

Compared to the beggar or anyone in a precarious situation, the king, the banker or the entrepreneur can say that they have succeeded in life, because they have managed to acquire a social status much higher than the beggar.

On the other hand, as far as romantic relationships are

concerned, both categories face the same difficulties. They all need to feel loved, appreciated and admired. All need to be loved as much as they need to drink and eat. In this field, they are all equal.

The tragedy of modern society we live in, is that we all aspire to meet our primary needs because they are imperative, but we do not know how to recognize and fulfill our emotional needs.

7. Love and dependence: living together.

The problem with attraction and romantic relationships is that you feel like a prisoner of the person you love. Indeed, we depend on the loved one to fulfill our emotional needs.

We always want this loved person to call us and show us signs of affection. But at the same time, we are upset and we are ashamed to feel this need. We would like to be free from this vulnerability, free from this desire to be loved in return, and free from this desire to be reassured that the relationship is a reciprocal one.

We are ashamed to feel this need for reciprocity because we find it degrading and humiliating. It puts us in a state of dependence, which we want to avoid at all costs. Basically, we would like to keep control of the situation and our feelings. But with the feeling of love, the emotional state becomes intense, and we lose the control of the situation. We feel lost.

We are angry against ourselves, and we resent the loved one for making us feel so desperate. We cannot bear the fact that our happiness depends on one person. We are angry toward ourselves for this lack of independence; meanwhile, we still resent her/him because he/she doesn't comfort us about it. Thus, we find ourselves in a situation where we hate the two beings who are the most precious to us: ourselves and the person who attracts us.

What to do then when we aspire to freedom, independence and autonomy, while our nature has designed us with emotional needs, which make us dependent to those we love?

8. Can we reconcile dependence and independence?

Take the example of a pretty young, free and independent woman, capable to provide for her own basic and material needs. The kind of young woman does not "need" anyone. This image is generally considered sexy and cool. Imagine when this woman falls in love with an attractive and independent man. Once in a relationship, she will "need" a little attention from her lover to feel fulfilled. If her lover does not show her some little mark of attention (a call, a little message, etc.), she will feel unhappy and scold him, because he didn't try to make any contact with her during the day. A call from him would have made her smile; a little "I love you" would have made her happy for the rest of the day.

Now, our independent young woman has fallen into the romantic trap. She now depends on another person to feel happy. She resents the fact that she "depends" emotionally on this man. She is forced to admit that she "needs" his calls to feel good. She is angry because it seems to her that it is not reciprocal. This man does not give her the impression that he "needs" her calls to feel good. She hates herself and she hates him too. She resents him for falling into the trap.

Keep in mind that we love free and independent heroes. What attracted her in the beginning was precisely that he gave her the impression he didn't need her. She found his independence and freedom sexy and cool. And now that she is with the hero, she resents him for not calling her all day long. She also resents him for not meeting all her emotional needs.

In the end, the reasons that attracted her to this man are the same that make her unhappy now. She wants him to be a little more attentive. However, if he had been more caring from their first meeting, she would have found him too available and accessible, and therefore less interesting. If he had been very caring from the start, she would not be with him right now. She would have thought that he needed her, and she would have gone hunting for other more interesting, more challenging and more exciting men. It is a vicious cycle…

Where do we get this tendency to run and get away from people who are accessible, available and ready to love us? Why are we fleeing, almost automatically, those who are ready and willing to offer us the love we seek so much? Why do we think we always deserve better than the person willing and ready to love us?

Chapter 3: Attraction Pull Factors Based on Superficial or Moral Values.

Sometimes, in order to look good, we claim that we are attracted by the moral values of the individuals we see or meet. But in reality, what criteria do people use to judge an anonymous person they have just met in an evening or on an online chat?

The answer to this question can upset or challenge our worldview. But it is essential because it helps to understand why we give opportunities to some individuals and not to others.

Psychologists agree in general that when we meet someone for the first time, we unconsciously ask ourselves two questions: Can I trust this person? Can I respect this person?

Indeed, every time we meet a new person, we wonder if she really deserves our trust and respect. It is the answers given to these two questions that determine the attitude we are going to have towards this unknown person. Given that we have limited means to assess the degree of trust and respect we can attribute to him/her, we have no choice but to rely on our instinct.

All means are good. We go through a zoom to evaluate them. We scan his/her clothes, shoes, haircut, smile, accent, appearance, pace, tone of voice, etc. It is by evaluating all these indicators that we internally decide the attitude to adopt.

But basically, what meaning do we give to these two words? What do we really mean by trust and respect?

In terms of interpersonal relationships, trust is usually defined by a spontaneous or acquired belief in the moral, emotional and professional value of another person, which makes us incapable of imagining from one's part deception, treason or incompetence.

Respect, on the other hand, is defined by a feeling that encourages someone to treat someone with respect and consideration because of their age, social position, value or worth.

1. Trust.

In general, the trust we place in people we have just met depends on the similarities we find in them. We have in us a kind of internal radar that pushes us to look for common traits with the other. These common points will make us trust him/her. The more we find, the more we are inclined to trust him/her because it make us feel comfortable and closer.

For example, at a party, young children will tend to play with other children of the same age group. Adults, too, will do the same and converse with other adults. The ladies will speak more easily between them, and men will be more at ease with other men.

Let's take a more powerful example. During a trip to Africa, a Japanese will be more likely to trust another Japanese he just met, even though they would never have noticed each other at home in Japan. Indeed, when we are far from home, we are more likely to trust those who share our origins and our language, because we believe that we share the same values or the same worldview. The best known example is that of two American tourists who meet in Paris; one of them could advise restaurants or places to visit and the second would have more confidence in his tastes and preferences because he thinks they share the same worldview.

These similarities, which make us trust someone, can take many forms. They can be the sharing of the same language, the same color of skin, values, a religion or a common belief system, or simply the sharing of the same origins. For example, we can automatically think that someone will never betray us simply because we share the same religious beliefs or the same worldview.

The selection criteria on which we base our degree of

openness and trust towards a stranger also depends on the context or the situation in which we find ourselves.

For example, in some American states, a young black will have little confidence in a white man in a police uniform. He might even fear for his life, especially if the interaction takes place at night with no witnesses around. Meanwhile, a white young man will feel comfortable interacting with anyone wearing a police uniform, whether it's a black or white officer anytime of the day.

2. Respect.

The respect we have for strangers heavily depends on our values and belief system. The environment in which we have evolved determines the degree of respect we will give to an unknown person.

For example, some cultures give a lot of respect to the elderly. They teach their children to treat the older ones with great care while other cultures give more respect to the soldiers who are fighting for their country. They arouse a nationalist or patriotic feeling, and the sight of these men and women in uniform inspires them with a form of unity and pride for their country. Other cultures tend to respect or denigrate someone according to their origins. For example, the class system in India determines the level of respect for an individual according to his caste of origin. Their social order is thus conceived.

Modern culture, highly influenced by a capitalist vision, tends to amplify the "merits" of the individual. In the United States, for example, the self-made man is seen as the hero of modern times, especially if he/she comes from a poor family and has built a financial empire from scratch. The media presents them as role models for society, and encourages all citizens to follow the same path.

Initially, we evaluate strangers through their appearance. It is their appearance that determines the level of trust and respect.

But beyond appearance, how do we evaluate the level of trust or respect?

3. The "annoying" social question: "What do you do for a living?"

At parties or in an online chat, when we first start talking with someone, one of the first questions we ask is, "What do you do for a living." This question gives us an idea of how much trust and respect we can give to the person.

We use this question as a scanner in our heads. The answer given determines whether this stranger worth importance, and if we need to get a little more involved with him/her in the conversation. What this person does in life seems to play an important role in our imagination. We find the stranger more or less interesting, depending on how he/she earns a living.

I know you probably think it's immoral, that people should be judged on their moral values, their honesty, their loyalty, their character, and so on. You think people should not judge someone according to one's work or profession. I am aware this thinking is inconvenient because it goes against the idea that we should judge the moral values of the individual, not his/her occupation.

Although this is embarrassing, let's think about the reasons why the: "So, what do you do in life? Is always the first and same question that always comes to our lips whenever we meet someone for the first time? Why don't the first set of questions asked when we meet a new person concern their belief in God, their political opinion, their musical tastes, their family relations, and so on?

We don't ask them these questions simply because they don't answer the first two questions that haunt us about trust and respect. Of course, we will ask them many more questions a little later, if the conversation goes on. But obviously, it is their occupation that gives us a real idea of the value we can give them.

Basically, we ask this question because, according to the prevailing capitalist system, the occupation or the professional career reveals sufficient clues from the stranger we have just met. It allows us to know if we want to go further with them, or if we should be wary. For example, if you discover the person holds a position with high responsibilities, it will indicate that he/she has won the trust of others, since he/she holds a prestigious position. The company in which he/she works will also give you an idea about the level of his/her salary. Finally, through his/her work and his/her responsibilities, you will have an idea about his/her level of education and the degree he/she has obtained.

On the other hand, if the stranger happens to be an independent artist - photographer, painter, writer or a musician - you will probably find them courageous and quite confident. You may think that they are a bit original, marginal or a bit poetic inside. You would also think they are a misfit, who has a hard time with not getting enough encouragement from their close relatives. You would tend to believe they cannot make a living through their art, and they have trouble making ends meet.

Conversely, if the stranger is a student, his field of study will show you what his passions and ambitions are. You would then think he is young and that he still has a bright future ahead of him/her. For example, the reputation of his university will give you clues about the financial means of his parents. In case he received a scholarship, you will conclude that his intelligence is quite above average.

Finally, if the stranger is a police officer or a soldier, you would conclude that he is disciplined and structured, that he has a stable salary and a promising career. You will already consider calling him in case of trouble.

Through my personal and professional experiences, I have been able to distinguish the types of personalities who attract each other the most. Most often, we seek in the others what we don't have. The one who has financial stability seeks the one who has independence; most of the time stability comes at the price of lot of obligations to fulfill. The one who has a well-paid job without much stimulation is looking for one who does creative work.

In conclusion, when you meet your in-laws for the first time, or a beautiful stranger, and they ask you this disturbing question - "So what do you do for a living?" - remember that your answer will initially determine the level of interest they will have for you. Their attitude towards you will be dramatically influenced by the answer you give.

Chapter 4: Logistical Attraction Pull Factors.

By interpersonal attraction, we refer to the positive feelings we feel towards another person. These feelings can take many forms: falling in love, becoming friends, enjoying, desiring or admiring someone. What happens when two people are attracted to each other? What are the factors that come into play?

In this chapter, I will introduce you to the 9 factors that drive attraction in an interpersonal relationship. I grouped them into 4 main categories: 1) physical attraction 2) similarity, 3) proximity, and 4) self-interest.

1. The physical attraction.

a. Physical beauty.

Different studies on human behavior show that, in general, we perceive "beautiful" people as being luckier, smarter, more open, kinder, well-intentioned, ready to act for the benefit of all, gentler and even more interesting. The participants in different tests also perceive "handsome" people as having fewer problems, with a more interesting career, living a good marriage and more successful in their life in general. These results show that we maintain biases and stereotypes based solely on people's physical appearance.

This goes beyond mere prejudices. In fact, other studies show that babies spend more time looking at "beautiful" people than looking at people perceived as less beautiful. You may think that an experience with babies does not really reflect the reality of the adult world. I agree with you, and that's why I'm going to tell you about another experiment with adults, in public, not in a laboratory.

The following experiment took place in New York during rush hour. Researchers had artificially disfigured the people who were being studied. They had made them look uglier, through Hollywood-like makeup, creating scars, lengthening or narrowing some parts of the face, and so on. The idea was to observe how people would react.

What were the results of the study in your opinion? Nobody, I repeat "nobody" wanted to sit next to these artificially disfigured people. Their skin color or age group didn't matter.

With the result of this research, it is easy to understand why people with beautiful physical traits are more likely to attract potential candidates for a romantic relationship. But some caution is needed here because, it must be remembered, physical beauty strongly depends on cultural criteria. Not everyone is looking to live with the most beautiful person in the world.

b. The same level of physical beauty.

Basically, we are looking for someone who is similar to us. We want to pair with someone who reflects the idea of our physical appearance.

If, for example, we give ourselves a score of 6 out of 10 for our physical appearance, we will tend to look for a partner with about the same rating, that is to say, one to whom we would also grant a 6/10. If we choose a partner with a much lower or much higher score, we will feel less satisfied in our relationship.

Indeed, if we judge that our partner deserves a score of 3/10, we will tend to think that we deserve better. If, on the other hand, we feel that our partner deserves a score of 9/10, we will not feel safe in our relationship. We will tend to have an inferiority complex, or we will develop an excessive jealousy that will make us believe that everyone wants our partner, and that he/she will leave us as soon as he/she meets a person of the same level.

Of course, our degree of attraction and the rating we award are done according to our own conception of beauty. We can give a 2/10 to a person while others give him/her a good 9/10, and vice versa. We tend to pair with a person whose physical traits make us as comfortable as possible.

However, the question about physical appearance does not stop there. Physical attraction is, in fact, an indispensable factor of attraction.

c. Physical attraction.

Concretely speaking, there must be some form of sexual attraction between the two individuals. Regardless of its intensity, frequency, or duration, both individuals must physically attract each other.

2. Similarity.

a. Share the same worldview.

Other studies of human behavior show that we tend to love the company of people who are like us, but not just physically. For example, if we enjoy a quiet, laid-back life, we will tend to avoid surrounding ourselves with a person who fuels drama. If we are afraid of taking risks, we will not surround ourselves with someone who likes extreme sports or gambling.

Our worldview is defined by a multitude of questions: How important is family to us? Are we looking for someone who is integrated or marginal? How important is friendship to him? Is it someone who knows how to keep his humbleness even in a moment of victory? Is she honest? Is she someone who likes to travel and discover new places? Is he an open-minded person?

The real answer to these questions, and not the one we give in public to project a certain self-image of ourselves, determines which people attract us.

But of course, we don't start a romantic relationship with everyone who thinks like us. The presence of another element is decisive: reciprocity.

b. Reciprocal liking.

We tend to like back the people who love us. It is a kind of mirror effect, the law of retaliation, "an eye for an eye, and a tooth for a tooth." We think those who love us arc grcat people. Conversely, we are convinced that those who do not love us are stupid and blind people who have not yet realized how good we are.

We tend to act in a positive way towards a person when we think that someone likes us. He will act the same way in return.

Beyond sharing the same worldview and reciprocal liking, there is one last attraction factor related to similarity: the exclusion criteria.

c. Exclusion criteria.

We all have a small list of qualities or characteristics we would like to find in our potential future partner before we commit. These are called our exclusion criteria.

For example, we may wish our future partner doesn't smoke, or we may want them to be okay with the fact that we smoke. We can wish that she has no children, or that she does not want to have children. We can hope that he has a lot of money, a certain level of education, a certain ethnic origin, religious belief, and so on.

Generally, the longer the list of exclusion criteria, the more difficult it will be to find a corresponding person. It is therefore necessary to avoid increasing the qualities or characteristics required.

Let's discuss attraction pull factors related to proximity.

3. The proximity.

a. The quality of interaction.

In order to appreciate someone, they must be somehow "near "physically or virtually. This is rather logical; otherwise, how could the two individuals meet?
In fact, it is easier for us to love a person with whom we regularly interact, who is part of our physical environment, and with whom we have to deal on a regular basis. Instinctively, we are suspicious of anyone outside our inner circle, or to whom we have never spoken. Thus, a classmate, a neighbor, a fellow church goer, a colleague, etc., inspires us to trust them more than a stranger.
Interaction accelerates attraction, but exposure plays a more important role.

b. Exposure.

The more we are exposed to something, the more we end up enjoying it over time. This is probably the reason why radios play the same song in a loop for a certain period of time. Even if we don't like this song in the beginning, we usually end up enjoying it more and more, although in some extreme cases, we end up hating it completely. Still, being exposed to something does not leave us indifferent, and that's what's important.

Among romantic relationships, we hear of many stories of people ending up together, whereas at first, they did not like each other. In this case, it is exposure that has favored the attraction factor.

Finally, the last attraction factor related to proximity is the anticipation of a future interaction.

c.   Anticipating a future interaction.

During a psychology study, researchers showed pictures of individuals to a group of students. They then had to determine which of these individuals were cataloged as "interesting." For the first group of students, the researchers simply showed pictures and then asked the students to rate the level of attractiveness of the individuals. For the second group, the researchers informed the students that some of these people lived in the same city or nearby. The second group noted the individuals significantly more positively than the first group.

What can we conclude from this study? We tend to judge more positively the people we might potentially come across in the future. This positive judgment is a kind of speculation about the future interactions we will have with these people.

Finally, the last factor of attraction, and perhaps the most important, is self-interest.

4. Personal interest.

Which partner do we think we deserve according to our social status, our achievements, our position, etc.? This is a practical question, which is a little taboo, but it is one that everyone asks himself at a given moment. We sometimes think, "I've been dating this person for a long time. Should I expect someone better?

Does this person meet my expectations? Are there other more interesting alternatives? Will they be accessible and interested in me? What would be the price to pay to get them?"
The answers to these questions we all ask ourselves at a given moment will determine the final choice of our partner.

THIRD PART:

THE DIFFERENT TYPES OF LOVE IN RELATIONSHIPS.

Chapter 1: The 3 Keys for understanding romantic relationships.

To better understand a relationship, one has to analyze it from three main angles: a) passion, b) intimacy, and c) commitment.

1. Passion.

The physical and sexual attraction between two partners is the main element in Hollywood scenarios or Western hits. The ideal partner must exert on us a physical attraction that transports us and makes us desire it constantly.

2. Intimacy or complicity.

Beyond physical attraction, the ideal couple loves to spend time together. The partners play, have fun and communicate a lot. Their complicity is unparalleled, they enjoy exclusive privacy, have no secrets to each other, do not judge each other, and share their joys and sorrows. In summary, they are true friends-lovers.

3. Commitment.

The third key for understanding love is commitment. The ideal couple engages in the relationship over the long term. The two individuals support each other, are supportive and generous to each other, and help each other to cope with the difficulties of life. In summary, each partner knows he can count on the other one in the long run.

4. The importance of these 3 components.

Here are, in a few words, the three main components of love. There are different combinations of these components that give different styles of relationship. It is through these keys that we can understand why we can be sexually attracted to a certain person while remaining in love and attached to someone else. It can also help us understand why the Western model often results in failures, separations and divorces.

Indeed, the model, which was proposed to us by modern society mostly from the Western world implies an exclusive relationship that includes these three elements - physical attraction, complicity and long-term commitment. The problem with this model is exclusivity and duration. The Western model is overly optimistic. It puts a lot of expectations on the partner, and catastrophizes when one of the three elements is not achieved.

It is rare that a relationship contains these 3 components from the first days. Relationships are developed and relationship styles differ from different socio-economic contexts.

In the following chapters, we will discuss the different styles of relationship, following the combination of these 3 keys - passion, intimacy and commitment.

Chapter 2: Commitment Contexts.

The different combinations of the 3 keys that make up a relationship can help us understand the type of relationship we are in.

1. The relationship without love.

A relationship without love is a relationship that does not include any of these 3 components. There is no physical attraction, no sharing of secrets, no commitment to each other. For example, the relationship I have with you, my readers, is a relationship without love. We cannot say that we are in a special relationship, we do not share our intimate secrets, we are not physically attracted, and we are not engaged with each other; we are complete strangers.

2. Empty love or the marriage of convenience.

Relations of this type of "empty-love" only consider duration. The only thing both partners take into account is a long-term commitment.

In some cultures in Africa and Asia, one marries to preserve the interests of the family or simply to acquire and/or maintain a certain social status. In these cases, the relationship with the partner will be almost like a business relationship; the partners are together to protect mutual interests. These interests are mostly their finances, their properties, their power of influence in the community, their prestige, and so on.

The reasons upon which the families of these individuals are based can be summed up in three simple words: power, popularity, and material wealth.

The link between their interests will be their offspring. The children will be the guarantors of their unity and the inheritors of their assets; they too are supposed to do everything in their power to ensure the sustainability of these assets.

In this kind of relationship, you do not have to feel physically attracted to your partner. There is no passion; there are only interests to protect or acquire.

And if we happen to be attracted by someone else?

In this case, the idea is to avoid scandals at all costs, always in the perspective of preserving common interests. The two partners don't share secrets (meaning they are not intimate or complicit) and do not desire each other; they see the sexual interaction as a duty to fulfill to procreate and maintain their privileges.

This type of relationship often applies to people who come from privileged or very conservative families.

a. Social responsibilities

For example, when a girl who is from a very conservative environment becomes pregnant outside marriage, her family will put pressure on the child's future father to get the two of them married in order to save the family's honor. This will be what can be considered a "marriage of reason/convenience," and the reason for this union is the honor of the girl's family. The two individuals are not ready to live a relationship and this child came somehow by "accident." That is to say, they did not plan to have it, but social obligations push them to take responsibility and engage in a long-term relationship in order to "save" the honor of the family first and maybe secondly the well-being of the child.

b. Social prestige

Another case can happen when one or both partners mutually choose to marry or be in a relationship without any family or social pressure, simply because they come from the same social background. They get together because they know it meets the expectations of their respective relatives.

In this case, it's always the same: the two partners maintain an appearance of happiness and stability and play some sort of comedy of love to show off. But basically, both individuals know they are together for interest.

c.   The weight of age

The last case that is by far the most common in this type of relationship, is the one that happens when someone is ready to engage only because the weight of age begins to feel heavy or simply because they feel "ready" financially or because social pressures are becoming untenable. When everyone around tells them that it is "time" or long overdue, in this case, the person concerned will do everything to look for and quickly find a partner to save face. Example?

The most obvious example is the case of a 35-year-old girl called Helene, who committed in a "serious" relationship with a "stable" and "funny" guy, whom we will call Steve. At the beginning of the relation-ship, in less than a month, Helene started telling Steve she wanted to have children with him, that he was the man of her life, and other similar statements. This left the impression that she wanted to have a long-term relationship with him. Steve got excited and moved in to live with her. But after two weeks together, Steve felt that something was wrong with Helene.

d.   What was wrong?

The problem is that she regularly cheated on him with her ex, whom we will call Richard. Basically, Helene would have preferred to engage with Richard, but he was unwilling to have a long-term relationship, or maybe if he wanted to have a long-term relationship, it wasn't certainly with her. Helene did everything to convince Richard, she sacrificed everything to achieve it, but unfortunately for her, he was only interested in two components of the relationship: (1) passion, that is to say, sex and physical attraction and (2) intimacy.

When Helene felt the weight of the age, she decided to get together with Steve and have at least someone who wanted to marry her and have kids with her (commitment), while still being physically attracted to Richard.

These cases are very common; some people get married only because it is "time" and because the person they desired and sought after did not want to make a long-term commitment with them for one reason or another. This is for example the case of a girl who will adopt the strategy to marry a man who has a "stable financial situation" and will remain in a secret relationship with her ex who was not rich enough to marry her.

These new cases of "marriage of individual convenience/ reason" are very common in Africa. The only difference is that, this time, the reason or the interest to preserve is not the interest of the family or the community, but rather an individual interest that is only known by one of the two partners.

For traditional weddings, both partners get married under pressure from family and really know what to expect; they have no illusions. While in the case of a marriage of "individual convenience/reason," one of the partners will necessarily feel deceived because she ignores what motivated the other to engage.

If you don't want to live an "empty-love" style of relationship without your knowledge, and if you don't want to feel played like a fool, one way to avoid this is to carefully study the past of this person who wants to engage so quickly with you...

Chapter 3: Passionate Love or Infatuation.

This type of love corresponds more to what we see in Hollywood-style scenarios. It is when one falls in love, when one feels one's belly gurgle at the sight of the loved person, when one finds the other perfect physically, without any defect, and that an irresistible force pushes us towards this person. When we see this person, we are literally inflamed and completely lose our mind, we are as subjugated by this person and believe that we could not live without her. We live her absence like a torture, we miss her nonstop, and live in a constant state of excitement and fear.

When it is reciprocal, we are overwhelmed by a feeling of euphoria, then we start to completely panic on the idea of being rejected by this person and we enter in a full anxiety mode when there is a small distance. Our senses are constantly stimulated, we fail to manage all these emotions of joys, fear, euphoria, excitement, panic, anxieties and uncertainties that invade us all the time. We lose control and feel completely naked and fragile in front of her; we live only to see her again. Nothing matters to us; only the loved one counts for us. We lose ourselves completely in the other person's world; we merge and we lose sense of time.

It is this emotional state that is often considered by Hollywood script to be love. And many people start a committed relationship on the basis of this feeling. They say to themselves that if they feel this feeling towards each other, it is a proof that they are made to live together, that they were created for each other and that their love will last forever.

This idea of starting a long-term relationship because one is infatuated with someone follows the Western model, and it is unfortunately the source of several disillusions and divorces. The first reason is that this feeling of euphoria lasts on average 3 years, the longest duration being 7 years.

If we engage with someone only because we have "fallen in love," but we do not take the time to feed this feeling that has a very limited lifespan, we risk separating once we no longer "feel" anything for the partner. Or in another case, we will leave him because we have just felt the same feeling of euphoria towards another person.

It is very dangerous to engage solely on the basis of a loving feeling, because we will all experience it for many people in our lives, but we are not obliged to marry these people anytime that feeling comes. It is downright irresponsible and illusory to want to make a long-term commitment every time we feel this short-lived feeling toward another person.

Imagine the case of a young adult named Elvis who is marrying a young girl (Grace) who has just made him feel euphoric and then, after a few years, say a six-year period, Elvis wants to leave Grace simply because he does not "feel" anything for her anymore, and he has "fallen in love" with another again. It's fine for Elvis, but at the same time, it's sad for the poor woman he leaves with his two children they had during the six years of living together. It's even sadder because Elvis could eventually still "fall in love" with another woman again. All his life, he will be constantly looking for someone who makes him feel this "special feeling" and each time, he will start a new relationship.

There are other cases where the two partners simply leave each other because they no longer feel this feeling towards each other. She will tell him, "There is nothing between us," and she will look to get this feeling of euphoria and excitement elsewhere.

Another cause of failure in this kind of relationship is that very often the two lovers forget to take into account the practical aspects of life together because they think the passion that drives them will be the only driving force of the relationship. As a result, they completely neglect the real needs of life and change their priorities to 180 degrees, but as we say, "we do not live for love and pink water."

It is necessary to learn how to calmly deal with money issues and practical life, because they often become a source of tension that the two lovers cannot manage, especially since they are not enough accomplices and intimate to be able to face certain difficulties.

The most common cases of this type of relationship solely focused on sexual attraction are found more often among those who are married or engaged in a lasting relationship who want to have a little fun without jeopardizing their already existing and boring relationship.

There are several cases in this type of relationship.

1. To reassure oneself about one's own power of seduction.

This will be the case, for example, of Aline, a 42-year-old woman married with three young children. She is a branch manager of an insurance company, and she feels her husband does not "look at her like before" and wants to feel like a woman again. She wants to feel that she can still seduce and awaken desire in someone. To achieve her desire, she will want to have a good time of pleasure with a young man who is still fresh enough to make her feel admired and appreciated again. The moments spent with this young man will be like a recreational moment that helps her escape the daily routine and heavy family and professional responsibilities. Of course she does not intend to leave her husband (see point 6, companion love), nor abandon her children. She only uses this young man to satisfy her sexual needs and to raise her self-esteem.

Generally, married men and women who indulge in that for this specific reason will actually do it during a trip or at a time when they are sure they cannot be "spotted."

2. To fulfill unmentionable fantasies.

Another very common case in Africa is that of a man called January. He is 35 years old and has been married for three years to Francine, a young woman of 29 years. January is a coordinator in an international NGO. He plays football on Saturday and attends church with his wife every Sunday. January's life looks stable and perfect, except for the fact that January has been dwelling in some so-called "dark" fantasies for some time, and he has a list of sexual games he dreams of doing.

The problem is he can't dare to talk to his wife, whom he finds very puritan and very religious. He likes the religious side of his wife, at least he is sure she would not cheat on him, but on the other side of the coin is that he is stuck in his personal growth and cannot talk to him about all his desires, which she would find "dirty" and weird.

Flooded by his desires, January will finally resort to finding a way of realizing them without the contribution of his wife. For that, he will be able to find a girl ready to do anything to please him, and it is with her that he will fulfill his secret and "dirty" desires. In this case, the sexual relationship between January and this young girl serves him to feel "accepted" and "received," which is to say this girl has just accepted his dark side that would have been criticized and judged by his wife, Francine. January is not ready to leave his wife he likes (see point 6, companion love), but he will maintain this other relationship based on sexual attraction with the girl who is ready to play his sexual games.

3. Revenge, distance and curiosity.

Sometimes one of the spouses will have an adulterous relationship out of curiosity, out of revenge, or to comfort him/herself of the distance imposed by the partner or the professional responsibilities.

Another very common case is that of young singles who are brought to see each other regularly. Let's say they are in the same social class, attend the same school or church, or are simply co-workers.

If both are free and do not have any significant person in their life, they would have a relationship based solely on sex to entertain themselves a bit, until one of them finds someone else to start a serious, committed relationship. Problems emerge when one of them begins to get emotionally attached to the other and wants more, seeking exclusivity and commitment.

There are many cases of people who have only pure physical desire among them, but there is one special case that is very rarely mentioned because it is taboo. This case concerns individuals who come to meet each other regularly because the context means they have no other alternatives. Over time, they will have to "desire" sexually a person who was not their first choice.

This is the case for people imprisoned for a long time. The harsh context they encounter in penitentiary environments, in which men are forced to live exclusively among themselves, gives them no access to the outside world. Some of them cannot bear the frustration and end up being attracted to other men while they were attracted to women in the beginning.

4. Conclusion.

Let us remember that 1. You must avoid engaging in a long-lasting relationship on the basis of this feeling of euphoria alone because it is of very short duration. 2. Know that when we are carried away by this feeling, we have a tendency to neglect or forget to take into account some essential and practical aspects of living in a relationship, and this can become a source of conflict and separation. We must find ways to maintain this feeling and learn to talk about the practical aspects of living together before embarking on a lasting relationship.

There is nothing more enjoyable than living this feeling and style of relationship with someone.

Chapter 4: The Relationship Centered on Friendship or Complicity.

In this type of relationship, the two partners love each other, and they love spending time together. They share their secrets, spend fun moments and support each other in difficult times. In short, they are real friends.

It is gratifying on an intimate level but it lacks the long-term aspect because both people are not planning to commit on an exclusive long-term relationship and do not physically attract each other. This relationship would be perfect if it stayed in the friendship realm. Everything changes when one of them wants more than the friendship.

You may know cases where someone falls in love with his friend, or maybe you've been in that yourselves already. This case happens so often that it's worth spending a little bit of time explaining it.

In order to understand a relationship of friends-lovers, let's first see what friendship is.

How can we define friendship?

It is a very vast subject and difficult to approach, but we can still define the concept of friendship with 4 essential points. These 4 points will allow you to understand your relations of friendship and their utility. Above all, they will help you understand why some people end up wanting to live in a relationship with their friends. Here are the 4 keys to understanding friendship:

1. A supportive network.

A friend is someone who uses his assets, knowledge or contacts to help us progress or improve our well-being. He is concerned about our advancement and puts it into practice as much as he can.

Deep down, we are all little fragile beings who evolve in a vast world that we have difficulties grasping. Our individual capacities are very limited, and these limits do not allow us to realize the many projects we have in our heads. It is clear that we cannot, despite all the determination of the world, achieve everything on our own without the help of anyone. We're not the movie heroes we discussed in the previous chapter; in reality, we all need someone to help us.

2. Share secrets and feel understood.

We all have dark sides and crazy ideas. These kinds of thoughts sometimes make us feel a little strange, weird or different than others.
What are these thoughts?
These are our regrets, resentments, unspeakable desires, ambitions, sexual compulsions, despair, confusions, etc. Basically, this is the kind of thought we would never dare to confess to anyone for fear of being criticized or judged.
We avoid talking about them and hide them in public and with those we know on a superficial level, because we are afraid to be considered mentally ill or crazy, and we do well to do so!
To feel less lonely, we need a friend who will make us feel normal despite all that. We need a friend who will admit to us that sometimes he also has some crazy and weird ideas that go through his head. By doing so, we will feel less alone and less crazy. This aspect of friendship allows us to be able to look in the mirror a little less harshly and with a little more compassion.

3. Have fun.

We live in a world in which people take themselves a little bit too seriously. We spend our days writing serious emails to our colleagues, sending invoices with serious big amounts, demanding serious increases for our salaries.

Then in the evening, we watch serious world news on serious channels that tell us about serious conflicts between serious countries, and these countries are fighting for serious interests and causes. Then after that, we have to seriously think about our weight and seriously tackle the issue with some exercises, starting a diet, or starting a profitable activity.

In short, at one point, we want to stop being serious and reasonable; we want to release the pressure and have a little fun. It is in this perspective that we need a friend who, despite his status as an architect, judge, senior executive, director in a large company, or other impressive title, will be there for us and will take time out to have fun and go crazy with us in a nightclub.

With her, we can feel okay with playing video games, or release the tension a little on a barbecue or a bottle of gin or by sharing any other entertaining activity and spending a pleasant moment together.

4. Have clear ideas.

Sometimes, we fail to think correctly; we are angry and we do not even know why. We are tormented without knowing where we get this feeling of anxiety; we have choices to make but lack some guidance or strategy to make the right decision.

A friend is the one who helps us see a little more

clearly in our lives. He will ask us simple and concise questions that will allow us to see more correctly and better approach the situation and solve our problems.

That's it for the 4 points of the friendship. It is rare to find a friend who meets these 4 criteria. They sometimes have one or at most three of these attributes. It is therefore not surprising that sometimes a friendship brings one of the two people to want a little more. And this "plus" is often expressed by desire and a certain form of sexual attraction, because among the four outlines of friendship, no mention is made of sexual attraction.

If the two friends start to physically be attracted to each other, it becomes a different type of relationship, which is called romantic love. (We will discuss it in the next point 5.)

5. Can we be friends with everyone?

In my opinion, it depends on the context but also which of these 4 points of friendship it is.

For example, it would be difficult for a married man or one engaged in a long-term relationship to maintain a deep friendship with a married woman, such as sharing secrets and feeling understood (point b) or having fun and doing crazy things together (point c). This kind of friendly relationship is not suitable and would cause jealousy and discomfort among their respective partners, especially since the two friends would eventually reveal intimate secrets of their couple that could hurt their partner. On the other hand, they could easily maintain a mutual supportive friendship (point a) or help each other have clear ideas (point b).

If it is a married person who is in a friendly relationship with a single person of the opposite sex, it could provoke jealousy of his partner if he had a friendly relationship style of type (b) (c) and (d).

In general, one should avoid having friendly relationships that arouse jealousy with the partner, for fear that she feel neglected or belittled. This could create misunderstandings that would propel the partner to make unrepairable mistakes. One has to learn how to choose friends who are beneficial to the couple, that is, those who serve in point (a) and (b), those who help you work more on your relationship, those who encourage you to stay together and those who help you progress in your respective careers.

Chapter 5: Romantic Love.

This type of relationship offers a fairly satisfying context for those who live it. Lovers are accomplices, share their secrets, emit more or less on the same wavelength, they physically desire each other, they rely on each other, they are very appreciative and can spend hours talking to each other or playing together. Everything looks beautiful in this kind of relationship; the only concern is that it lacks the "commitment" aspect.

In general, people who live this kind of relationship want to push further, but they cannot achieve it for several reasons. Here are some cases:

Let's take the example of Robert, a 23-year-old student who still lives in his parents' home and is still financially dependent on them for the rest of his studies. Robert is crazy in love with Krystle, a young and pretty 26-year-old girl who works for a telecom company. The two would like to live their lives together but unfortunately, Robert does not have the financial means to do it; he has to wait until the end of his studies and he is not even guaranteed that at the end of studies he will find a well-paying job.

The future of this couple is uncertain. Krystle would like to wait until Robert finds a better situation, but it could take him at least 5 years and by then, she doubts that Robert will still be in love with her. She is scared and has some doubts because she thinks at one point, he'll get tired and take another girl once he gets a job. In addition to this, she endures strong social pressure. She is always invited to the weddings of her close relatives, and her family is pressuring her to get married because she has everything to succeed: she comes from a good family, she has a good job, she is qualified, and she has a long list of other contenders who want to engage with her.

Both love each other but cannot blossom and live their relationship completely because the social context does not allow it. They will therefore opt for a brief romantic relationship, and Krystle will marry another man, Jean, a 33-year-old man who works in the banking sector and has a promising future. Robert will finish his studies and engage with Clarisse, a nice girl two years younger than him. Of course, the two lovers will continue to see each other in secret while thinking about the relationship they would have had if the circumstances had allowed.

Another case of romantic relationship is illustrated by

the relationships that young teenagers have. They will love each other passionately for a short period of time, either a school year or a trimester, until they get bored and move on to someone else. They will live happy and intense moments knowing that it is for a short time.

There are other cases where one of the two people is already engaged in another relationship. In this case, this person will live a romantic relationship with his lover or his mistress while preserving the integrity of his reputation and that of his family.

The case of Natacha is very expressive. Natacha is a 42-year-old woman who lives with her husband Richard, who is 45 years old. They have 3 children together and have been married for 12 years; they both have a good job, their kids go to school and they live in a nice neighborhood. Their life is rather calm, and they almost never quarrel, Richard is a rather relaxed man and not very demanding, and Natacha takes good care of the business of the house; the two have a rather quiet family life.

But here, Natacha hides a secret: ever since she was a teenager, she knew she was attracted to women. She has never dared to admit it to her family, but a few of her friends know her secret. She secretly sees Diane, another married woman. They get along well and love each other tenderly, but both hide their relationship to preserve their reputation and that of their children because this kind of subject is still taboo in African societies. If their relationship was revealed, the price to

pay would be too heavy, and it is not worth sacrificing everything for that. Sometimes in very particular
contexts, some relationships can only really be lived
in secret.

It is also possible to have a relationship in which
those who live it are intimate and engaged but do
there is no physical attraction. This type of relationship is called companion love.

Chapter 6: Companion Love.

In this type of relationship, both partners share their secrets, support each other, and are engaged to each other. They live a committed, long-term relationship but they are not attracted physically to each other anymore.

The cases vary in this type of relationship; it can vary between (1) those who were attracted at the beginning but the desire has eroded over time. They can never think of separating themselves so as not to destroy what they have built over the years: home, children, social prestige etc. Or (2) others who have never been attracted to each other. They live a marriage arranged by their parents but over time, they have come to appreciate each other, and they have developed a kind of intimacy through living together. Or simply (3) cases of couples who got together because they share the same ambitions and the same secrets.

In short, companion love is an empty love relationship in which the intimacy and complicity aspect is added.

Here is an example that illustrates this type of relationship.

Becky, a 26-year-old woman, and Eric, a 27-year-old, are two young people who have engaged in a lasting relationship and ended up getting married because they shared the same secret and the same ambitions.

Both had a master's degree and wanted to succeed in life. They were determined to have brilliant international careers and were ready to do anything to achieve this. They had a common obstacle: they were both gay, and neither wanted to confront their own family to open up and discuss about the issue. When they met, they developed a beautiful friendship, continued to see each other and finally disclosed their secrets to each other.

Both were handsome, young and privileged. They knew their respective families would appreciate their union. So, they decided to get married to achieve their ambitions and to live their secret more easily. In their case, everyone protects and helps the other; they are engaged in a long-term relationship devoid of any passion and desire.

CONCLUSION

Here is what the three parts of this book helped us understand and what it can serve us.
In the first part, we saw the main, often unrealistic expectations that we feed on the supposed qualities of the ideal spouse. This allowed us to reduce the pressure and judge our (future) partner less harshly. He may not be perfect, but we have learned to be less judgmental and appreciate what we have. We have understood that modern society shapes frustrated individuals, through the various advertisements that always promise new objects, always better than those we already have. We have also seen where this unfortunate tendency to neglect those who attach themselves to us comes from. We understand that anything that is valuable is not necessarily rare, at least in terms of romantic relationships.
In the second part, we made the difference between fantasies and reality. This part helped us understand why some people have an almost irresistible appeal to

us, and how our social environment has shaped us to be attracted to such people. We have also understood our criteria of judgment are, when it comes to partner choice.

Finally, the third part allowed us to know in which type of relationship we are or which we are looking for. It helped us to better position ourselves. For example, if you live in a relationship that includes only passion and commitment, without the intimacy aspect, it's up to you to determine what kind of relationship you want, and work to fill in what's missing. In case you are living a passionate one-way relationship, you should think about how you could develop the passion aspect in your partner. The idea is not to judge the state of your relationship. It is up to you to see what is missing, so that you can live a complete love if, of course, you wish to live this type of relationship.

A style of relationship which is complete love, that is to say which contains the 3 components of a relationship (commitment, passion and intimacy), would be the ideal, but it requires you to really work its relationship. This is exactly what will be discussed in the next book. I will give you the keys and tips to achieve a full love relationship.